EMMANUEL JOSEPH

Beyond the Balance Sheet, The Hidden Lives of Those Who Shape the World

Copyright © 2025 by Emmanuel Joseph

All rights reserved. No part of this publication may be reproduced, stored or transmitted in any form or by any means, electronic, mechanical, photocopying, recording, scanning, or otherwise without written permission from the publisher. It is illegal to copy this book, post it to a website, or distribute it by any other means without permission.

First edition

This book was professionally typeset on Reedsy.
Find out more at reedsy.com

Contents

1	Chapter 1: The Visionary Dreamers	1
2	Chapter 2: The Unsung Heroes	3
3	Chapter 3: The Ethical Innovators	5
4	Chapter 4: The Relentless Problem-Solvers	7
5	Chapter 5: The Courageous Risk-Takers	9
6	Chapter 6: The Quiet Strategists	11
7	Chapter 7: The Resilient Survivors	13
8	Chapter 8: The Inspirational Leaders	15
9	Chapter 9: The Creative Innovators	17
10	Chapter 10: The Humble Innovators	19
11	Chapter 11: The Persistent Advocates	21
12	Chapter 12: The Respected Mentors	23
13	Chapter 13: The Fearless Entrepreneurs	25
14	Chapter 14: The Collaborative Team Players	27
15	Chapter 15: The Tech Pioneers	29
16	Chapter 16: The Community Builders	31
17	Chapter 17: The Legacy Makers	33

1

Chapter 1: The Visionary Dreamers

In the world of finance, we often focus on numbers and profits, but behind these figures are visionary dreamers who dare to challenge the status quo. These individuals possess an uncanny ability to foresee trends and opportunities before they materialize. They are the ones who envision a future that others cannot yet see. Their stories are not just about financial success but about the passion, determination, and resilience that drive them to turn their dreams into reality. From Silicon Valley tech moguls to Wall Street titans, these dreamers shape the world by pushing the boundaries of innovation and daring to dream big.

Their journeys are rarely smooth, often filled with setbacks and challenges that test their resolve. Yet, it is their unwavering belief in their vision that sets them apart. They understand that failure is not the end but a stepping stone towards success. Through their stories, we learn the importance of perseverance and the willingness to take risks. These visionaries inspire us to think beyond the balance sheet and embrace the possibilities that lie ahead. Their hidden lives are a testament to the power of dreaming big and the impact that one person's vision can have on the world.

As we delve into their stories, we discover that their motivations go beyond financial gain. Many of them are driven by a desire to create something meaningful, to leave a lasting legacy that extends far beyond their lifetimes. They are not content with simply amassing wealth; they seek to make a difference in the world. Whether it's through philanthropy, innovation, or social change, these visionaries use their success to contribute to a greater good. Their hidden lives reveal a deeper purpose that transcends the confines of traditional business.

In this chapter, we explore the lives of some of the most influential visionaries of our time. Through their stories, we gain insights into the qualities that make them extraordinary. Their ability to dream, their resilience in the face of adversity, and their commitment to making a positive impact on the world are qualities that we can all aspire to. By looking beyond the balance sheet, we can uncover the hidden lives of those who shape the world and find inspiration in their remarkable journeys.

2

Chapter 2: The Unsung Heroes

While the spotlight often shines on CEOs and top executives, there is a multitude of unsung heroes who work tirelessly behind the scenes. These individuals are the backbone of organizations, ensuring that operations run smoothly and efficiently. From dedicated administrative staff to diligent IT professionals, their contributions are invaluable, yet they rarely receive the recognition they deserve. Their stories are a testament to the importance of teamwork and the crucial role that every individual plays in achieving success.

These unsung heroes often go unnoticed, but their impact is undeniable. They are the ones who keep the wheels turning, solving problems and finding solutions to ensure that everything runs seamlessly. Their dedication and hard work are what make it possible for the visionaries and leaders to shine. Without them, even the most brilliant ideas would struggle to come to fruition. Their hidden lives are filled with countless hours of effort, commitment, and a deep sense of pride in their work.

As we delve into the lives of these unsung heroes, we discover the unique challenges they face and the qualities that make them exceptional. Their stories remind us of the importance of recognizing and appreciating the contributions of every team member. In a world that often prioritizes individual achievements, it is essential to remember that success is a collective effort. By looking beyond the balance sheet, we can see the true value of these individuals and the vital role they play in shaping the world.

In this chapter, we celebrate the unsung heroes who work behind the scenes. Their stories offer a glimpse into the hidden lives of those who contribute to the success of organizations in ways that are often overlooked. Through their dedication and hard work, they make a significant impact on the world. By acknowledging and appreciating their contributions, we can foster a culture of teamwork and collaboration that benefits everyone.

3

Chapter 3: The Ethical Innovators

In a world driven by profit, there are those who choose to prioritize ethics and social responsibility. These ethical innovators are committed to creating positive change and making a difference in their communities. They understand that business success and social impact are not mutually exclusive but can go hand in hand. Their hidden lives are a testament to the power of doing good while doing well. From sustainable businesses to social enterprises, these individuals are redefining the purpose of business.

Ethical innovators face unique challenges as they navigate the complexities of balancing profit with purpose. They often encounter resistance and skepticism, yet their unwavering commitment to their values drives them forward. Their stories highlight the importance of integrity, transparency, and a genuine desire to make a positive impact. Through their efforts, they are changing the way we think about business and inspiring others to follow suit.

As we explore the lives of these ethical innovators, we gain insights into the qualities that set them apart. Their passion for making a difference, their dedication to ethical practices, and their innovative approaches to problem-solving are qualities that we can all admire. Their hidden lives reveal a deeper sense of purpose and a commitment to creating a better world for future generations. By looking beyond the balance sheet, we can see the profound impact that ethical innovators have on society.

In this chapter, we celebrate the ethical innovators who are shaping the world with their commitment to social responsibility. Their stories serve as a reminder that business can be a force for good, and that success is not measured solely by financial gain. By prioritizing ethics and social impact, these individuals are making a lasting difference in the world. Their hidden lives inspire us to consider the broader implications of our actions and to strive for a more just and equitable society.

4

Chapter 4: The Relentless Problem-Solvers

At the heart of every successful organization are relentless problem-solvers who thrive on challenges and obstacles. These individuals possess a unique ability to identify issues and develop creative solutions. Their hidden lives are characterized by a constant drive to improve and innovate. From engineers to researchers, these problem-solvers are the ones who turn ideas into reality and make the impossible possible. Their stories are a testament to the power of perseverance and the impact of innovative thinking.

Relentless problem-solvers often operate in the background, working tirelessly to overcome obstacles and find solutions. They are the ones who take on the toughest challenges and refuse to give up until they achieve success. Their dedication and determination are what set them apart. Through their stories, we learn the importance of resilience and the value of thinking outside the box. Their hidden lives reveal a deep-seated passion for solving problems and a commitment to making a difference.

As we delve into the lives of these relentless problem-solvers, we gain insights into the qualities that make them exceptional. Their ability to see opportunities where others see obstacles, their persistence in the face of setbacks, and their innovative approaches to problem-solving are qualities that we can all aspire to. Their stories remind us that challenges are not roadblocks but opportunities for growth and improvement. By looking beyond the balance sheet, we can uncover the hidden lives of those who shape the world through their relentless pursuit of solutions.

In this chapter, we celebrate the relentless problem-solvers who drive innovation and progress. Their stories offer a glimpse into the hidden lives of those who dedicate themselves to overcoming challenges and finding solutions. Through their efforts, they make a significant impact on the world. By recognizing and appreciating their contributions, we can foster a culture of innovation and problem-solving that benefits everyone.

5

Chapter 5: The Courageous Risk-Takers

Every groundbreaking achievement is the result of courageous risk-takers who dare to venture into the unknown. These individuals possess a fearless spirit and a willingness to take bold steps. Their hidden lives are marked by a series of calculated risks that often defy conventional wisdom. From entrepreneurs to investors, these risk-takers are the ones who propel industries forward and create new possibilities. Their stories are a testament to the power of courage and the impact of daring to take risks.

Courageous risk-takers often face uncertainty and skepticism, yet their belief in their vision drives them forward. They understand that great rewards often come from taking great risks. Through their stories, we learn the importance of embracing uncertainty and the value of calculated risk-taking. Their hidden lives reveal a deep-seated passion for pushing boundaries and challenging the status quo. By looking beyond the balance sheet, we can see the true value of those who dare to take risks.

As we explore the lives of these courageous risk-takers, we gain insights into the qualities that set them apart. Their ability to make bold decisions, their resilience in the face of setbacks, and their unwavering belief in their vision are qualities that we can all admire. Their stories inspire us to step out of our comfort zones and embrace the possibilities that lie ahead. By recognizing and appreciating the contributions of these risk-takers, we can foster a culture of innovation and progress.

In this chapter, we celebrate the courageous risk-takers who shape the world with their bold actions. Their stories offer a glimpse into the hidden lives of those who dare to venture into the unknown. Through their efforts, they make a significant impact on the world. By acknowledging and appreciating their contributions, we can encourage others to take risks and pursue their dreams.

6

Chapter 6: The Quiet Strategists

Behind every successful organization are quiet strategists who meticulously plan and execute long-term goals. These individuals may not always seek the spotlight, but their impact is profound. They are the ones who analyze market trends, develop innovative strategies, and ensure that the organization stays on the right track. Their hidden lives are filled with careful planning, analysis, and a deep understanding of the industry. From financial analysts to business consultants, these strategists shape the future with their calculated decisions.

Quiet strategists often work behind the scenes, making decisions that influence the direction of entire organizations. They possess a unique ability to see the big picture while paying attention to the smallest details. Their stories highlight the importance of strategic thinking and the value of thoughtful decision-making. Through their efforts, they help organizations navigate complex challenges and seize opportunities for growth.

As we delve into the lives of these quiet strategists, we gain insights into the qualities that make them exceptional. Their analytical minds, strategic vision, and ability to adapt to changing circumstances are qualities that we can all admire. Their hidden lives reveal a deep commitment to achieving long-term success and a dedication to making informed decisions. By looking beyond the balance sheet, we can uncover the hidden lives of those who shape the world through their strategic prowess.

BEYOND THE BALANCE SHEET, THE HIDDEN LIVES OF THOSE WHO SHAPE THE WORLD

In this chapter, we celebrate the quiet strategists who drive the success of organizations. Their stories offer a glimpse into the hidden lives of those who plan and execute strategies with precision. Through their efforts, they make a significant impact on the world. By recognizing and appreciating their contributions, we can foster a culture of strategic thinking and informed decision-making.

7

Chapter 7: The Resilient Survivors

In the world of business, resilience is a key trait that sets successful individuals apart. The resilient survivors are those who have faced adversity head-on and emerged stronger. Their hidden lives are marked by a series of challenges that test their resolve and determination. From economic downturns to personal setbacks, these individuals have navigated difficult circumstances with grace and perseverance. Their stories are a testament to the power of resilience and the impact of overcoming obstacles.

Resilient survivors often find themselves in situations that seem insurmountable. Yet, their ability to adapt and bounce back is what sets them apart. They understand that setbacks are a part of the journey and that success is not always a linear path. Through their stories, we learn the importance of resilience and the value of perseverance. Their hidden lives reveal a deep-seated strength and a commitment to pushing forward, no matter the challenges they face.

As we explore the lives of these resilient survivors, we gain insights into the qualities that make them exceptional. Their ability to adapt to changing circumstances, their determination in the face of adversity, and their unwavering belief in their potential are qualities that we can all aspire to. Their stories remind us that challenges are opportunities for growth and that resilience is a key component of success. By looking beyond the balance sheet, we can uncover the hidden lives of those who shape the world through their resilience.

In this chapter, we celebrate the resilient survivors who overcome obstacles and thrive in the face of adversity. Their stories offer a glimpse into the hidden lives of those who navigate challenges with grace and determination. Through their efforts, they make a significant impact on the world. By recognizing and appreciating their contributions, we can foster a culture of resilience and perseverance.

8

Chapter 8: The Inspirational Leaders

Inspirational leaders are those who motivate and guide others towards a common goal. Their hidden lives are characterized by their ability to inspire and influence those around them. From CEOs to team managers, these leaders possess a unique ability to connect with people and bring out the best in them. Their stories are a testament to the power of leadership and the impact of motivating others. Through their guidance, they shape the culture and success of organizations.

Inspirational leaders often lead by example, demonstrating the qualities they wish to see in others. They possess a deep understanding of human nature and the ability to empathize with their team members. Their stories highlight the importance of effective communication, trust, and the ability to inspire others to achieve their full potential. Through their efforts, they create a positive and productive work environment where everyone can thrive.

As we delve into the lives of these inspirational leaders, we gain insights into the qualities that make them exceptional. Their ability to connect with people, their dedication to developing others, and their commitment to creating a positive impact are qualities that we can all admire. Their hidden lives reveal a deep sense of purpose and a passion for helping others succeed. By looking beyond the balance sheet, we can see the profound impact that inspirational leaders have on their organizations and the world.

In this chapter, we celebrate the inspirational leaders who guide and motivate others towards success. Their stories offer a glimpse into the hidden lives of those who lead with empathy and vision. Through their efforts, they make a significant impact on the world. By recognizing and appreciating their contributions, we can foster a culture of leadership and inspiration that benefits everyone.

9

Chapter 9: The Creative Innovators

Innovation is the driving force behind progress, and creative innovators are the ones who push the boundaries of what is possible. These individuals possess a unique ability to think outside the box and develop groundbreaking ideas. Their hidden lives are filled with experimentation, creativity, and a relentless pursuit of new solutions. From inventors to artists, these innovators shape the future with their imaginative thinking. Their stories are a testament to the power of creativity and the impact of innovative ideas.

Creative innovators often challenge conventional wisdom and explore uncharted territories. They are the ones who see possibilities where others see limitations. Their stories highlight the importance of creativity and the value of embracing new perspectives. Through their efforts, they drive progress and bring about transformative change. Their hidden lives reveal a deep-seated passion for innovation and a commitment to making a difference.

As we explore the lives of these creative innovators, we gain insights into the qualities that set them apart. Their ability to think outside the box, their persistence in the face of challenges, and their willingness to take risks are qualities that we can all aspire to. Their stories remind us that creativity is a powerful tool for problem-solving and that innovative thinking can lead to remarkable achievements. By looking beyond the balance sheet, we can uncover the hidden lives of those who shape the world through their creativity.

In this chapter, we celebrate the creative innovators who drive progress and inspire change. Their stories offer a glimpse into the hidden lives of those who push the boundaries of what is possible. Through their efforts, they make a significant impact on the world. By recognizing and appreciating their contributions, we can foster a culture of creativity and innovation that benefits everyone.

10

Chapter 10: The Humble Innovators

While some innovators bask in the limelight, there are those who prefer to let their work speak for itself. These humble innovators often shy away from the spotlight, allowing their creations to take center stage. They are driven by a passion for problem-solving and a desire to make a difference, rather than seeking fame or recognition. Their hidden lives are filled with quiet dedication, creativity, and a relentless pursuit of excellence. From scientists to engineers, these humble innovators shape the world with their groundbreaking discoveries and inventions.

Humble innovators often work behind the scenes, making significant contributions without seeking credit. They are the ones who focus on the task at hand, driven by a genuine passion for their work. Their stories highlight the importance of humility and the value of letting one's work speak for itself. Through their efforts, they create solutions that have a lasting impact on society. Their hidden lives reveal a deep-seated commitment to making a difference and a dedication to the pursuit of knowledge.

As we delve into the lives of these humble innovators, we gain insights into the qualities that set them apart. Their humility, dedication, and unwavering commitment to their work are qualities that we can all admire. Their stories remind us that true innovation is driven by a desire to solve problems and make a positive impact, rather than seeking recognition or fame. By looking beyond the balance sheet, we can uncover the hidden lives of those who shape the world through their humble contributions.

In this chapter, we celebrate the humble innovators who make significant contributions without seeking the spotlight. Their stories offer a glimpse into the hidden lives of those who let their work speak for itself. Through their efforts, they make a significant impact on the world. By recognizing and appreciating their contributions, we can foster a culture of humility and dedication that benefits everyone.

11

Chapter 11: The Persistent Advocates

In the quest for social change, persistent advocates play a crucial role in raising awareness and driving progress. These individuals are committed to advocating for causes they believe in, often working tirelessly to bring about change. Their hidden lives are marked by a deep passion for social justice, equality, and human rights. From activists to community leaders, these advocates shape the world by giving a voice to the voiceless and fighting for a more just society. Their stories are a testament to the power of advocacy and the impact of persistence.

Persistent advocates often face resistance and challenges, yet their unwavering commitment to their cause drives them forward. They understand that meaningful change takes time and effort, and they are willing to put in the work to achieve their goals. Their stories highlight the importance of persistence and the value of standing up for what is right. Through their efforts, they bring attention to important issues and inspire others to take action.

As we explore the lives of these persistent advocates, we gain insights into the qualities that make them exceptional. Their passion for social justice, their dedication to their cause, and their resilience in the face of adversity are qualities that we can all aspire to. Their hidden lives reveal a deep sense of purpose and a commitment to making a positive impact on the world. By looking beyond the balance sheet, we can see the profound influence that persistent advocates have on society.

In this chapter, we celebrate the persistent advocates who fight for social change and justice. Their stories offer a glimpse into the hidden lives of those who dedicate themselves to advocating for important causes. Through their efforts, they make a significant impact on the world. By recognizing and appreciating their contributions, we can foster a culture of advocacy and social responsibility that benefits everyone.

12

Chapter 12: The Respected Mentors

Mentorship is a powerful tool for personal and professional growth, and respected mentors play a crucial role in guiding and nurturing the next generation of leaders. These individuals possess a wealth of knowledge and experience, and they are dedicated to sharing their insights with others. Their hidden lives are characterized by a deep commitment to helping others succeed. From teachers to coaches, these mentors shape the future by providing guidance, support, and encouragement. Their stories are a testament to the power of mentorship and the impact of investing in others.

Respected mentors often take on the role of advisor and confidant, offering valuable insights and guidance to those they mentor. They possess a unique ability to connect with people and provide personalized support. Their stories highlight the importance of mentorship and the value of fostering growth and development in others. Through their efforts, they create a positive and nurturing environment where individuals can thrive.

As we delve into the lives of these respected mentors, we gain insights into the qualities that make them exceptional. Their ability to listen, their dedication to developing others, and their commitment to making a positive impact are qualities that we can all admire. Their hidden lives reveal a deep sense of purpose and a passion for helping others succeed. By looking beyond the balance sheet, we can uncover the hidden lives of those who shape the world through their mentorship.

In this chapter, we celebrate the respected mentors who guide and nurture the next generation of leaders. Their stories offer a glimpse into the hidden lives of those who dedicate themselves to helping others succeed. Through their efforts, they make a significant impact on the world. By recognizing and appreciating their contributions, we can foster a culture of mentorship and support that benefits everyone.

13

Chapter 13: The Fearless Entrepreneurs

Entrepreneurship is a journey filled with risks and challenges, and fearless entrepreneurs are the ones who embrace the unknown with determination and courage. These individuals possess a unique ability to identify opportunities and turn them into successful ventures. Their hidden lives are marked by a relentless pursuit of their dreams, often overcoming significant obstacles along the way. From startup founders to small business owners, these entrepreneurs shape the world with their innovative ideas and unwavering drive. Their stories are a testament to the power of entrepreneurship and the impact of fearless determination.

Fearless entrepreneurs often face uncertainty and skepticism, yet their belief in their vision drives them forward. They understand that success is not guaranteed, but they are willing to take risks and learn from their failures. Their stories highlight the importance of resilience and the value of embracing challenges. Through their efforts, they create businesses that drive economic growth and innovation. Their hidden lives reveal a deep-seated passion for building something meaningful and a commitment to achieving their goals.

As we explore the lives of these fearless entrepreneurs, we gain insights into the qualities that set them apart. Their ability to identify opportunities, their determination in the face of challenges, and their willingness to take risks are qualities that we can all aspire to. Their stories remind us that entrepreneurship is a journey of continuous learning and growth. By looking beyond the balance sheet, we can uncover the hidden lives of those who shape the world through their entrepreneurial spirit.

In this chapter, we celebrate the fearless entrepreneurs who drive innovation and economic growth. Their stories offer a glimpse into the hidden lives of those who embrace the challenges of entrepreneurship. Through their efforts, they make a significant impact on the world. By recognizing and appreciating their contributions, we can foster a culture of entrepreneurship and innovation that benefits everyone.

14

Chapter 14: The Collaborative Team Players

Collaboration is essential for achieving success, and collaborative team players are the ones who bring people together to work towards a common goal. These individuals possess a unique ability to foster teamwork and create a positive and inclusive work environment. Their hidden lives are characterized by a deep commitment to working with others and a dedication to achieving collective success. From project managers to team leaders, these collaborative team players shape the world with their ability to build strong and cohesive teams. Their stories are a testament to the power of collaboration and the impact of working together.

Collaborative team players often take on the role of facilitator, ensuring that everyone has a voice and that diverse perspectives are considered. They understand the importance of communication, trust, and mutual respect. Their stories highlight the value of teamwork and the importance of fostering a collaborative environment. Through their efforts, they create a sense of unity and shared purpose that drives success. Their hidden lives reveal a deep-seated commitment to working with others and a passion for building strong teams.

As we delve into the lives of these collaborative team players, we gain insights into the qualities that make them exceptional. Their ability to foster teamwork, their dedication to creating an inclusive environment, and their commitment to achieving collective success are qualities that we can all admire. Their stories remind us that collaboration is a key component of success and that working together can lead to remarkable achievements. By looking beyond the balance sheet, we can uncover the hidden lives of those who shape the world through their collaborative efforts.

In this chapter, we celebrate the collaborative team players who drive success through teamwork and collaboration. Their stories offer a glimpse into the hidden lives of those who bring people together to achieve common goals. Through their efforts, they make a significant impact on the world. By recognizing and appreciating their contributions, we can foster a culture of collaboration and teamwork that benefits everyone.

15

Chapter 15: The Tech Pioneers

In the rapidly evolving world of technology, tech pioneers are the ones who lead the way with their innovative ideas and groundbreaking solutions. These individuals possess a unique ability to understand and leverage new technologies to create value and drive progress. Their hidden lives are filled with experimentation, creativity, and a relentless pursuit of technological advancement. From software developers to tech entrepreneurs, these pioneers shape the future with their visionary thinking. Their stories are a testament to the power of technology and the impact of pioneering innovation.

Tech pioneers often operate on the cutting edge, exploring new frontiers and pushing the boundaries of what is possible. They are the ones who see the potential of emerging technologies and find ways to apply them in practical and impactful ways. Their stories highlight the importance of staying ahead of the curve and the value of continuous learning and adaptation. Through their efforts, they drive technological progress and create solutions that transform industries. Their hidden lives reveal a deep-seated passion for innovation and a commitment to leveraging technology for the greater good.

As we explore the lives of these tech pioneers, we gain insights into the qualities that set them apart. Their ability to understand and leverage new technologies, their creativity in finding innovative solutions, and their dedication to driving technological progress, and their commitment to leveraging technology for the greater good are qualities that we can all admire. Their hidden lives reveal a deep-seated passion for innovation and a drive to create a better future.

As we explore the lives of these tech pioneers, we gain insights into the qualities that set them apart. Their ability to understand and leverage new technologies, their creativity in finding innovative solutions, and their dedication to driving progress are qualities that we can all aspire to. Their stories remind us that technology has the power to transform lives and shape the future. By looking beyond the balance sheet, we can uncover the hidden lives of those who shape the world through their technological advancements.

In this chapter, we celebrate the tech pioneers who lead the way with their innovative ideas and groundbreaking solutions. Their stories offer a glimpse into the hidden lives of those who drive progress and transform industries. Through their efforts, they make a significant impact on the world. By recognizing and appreciating their contributions, we can foster a culture of innovation and technological advancement that benefits everyone.

16

Chapter 16: The Community Builders

Community builders are the ones who bring people together and create a sense of belonging. These individuals possess a unique ability to connect with others and foster a sense of community. Their hidden lives are characterized by a deep commitment to building strong and supportive communities. From local leaders to social organizers, these community builders shape the world by creating spaces where people can come together and support one another. Their stories are a testament to the power of community and the impact of building connections.

Community builders often work behind the scenes, creating programs and initiatives that bring people together. They understand the importance of fostering a sense of belonging and the value of creating supportive environments. Their stories highlight the importance of community and the impact of building strong connections. Through their efforts, they create spaces where people can thrive and support one another. Their hidden lives reveal a deep-seated commitment to building strong and resilient communities.

As we delve into the lives of these community builders, we gain insights into the qualities that make them exceptional. Their ability to connect with others, their dedication to creating supportive environments, and their commitment to building strong communities are qualities that we can all admire. Their stories remind us that community is a powerful force for positive change and that building connections can lead to remarkable achievements. By looking beyond the balance sheet, we can uncover the hidden lives of those who shape the world through their community-building efforts.

In this chapter, we celebrate the community builders who create spaces for people to come together and support one another. Their stories offer a glimpse into the hidden lives of those who dedicate themselves to fostering a sense of community. Through their efforts, they make a significant impact on the world. By recognizing and appreciating their contributions, we can foster a culture of community and connection that benefits everyone.

17

Chapter 17: The Legacy Makers

Legacy makers are those who seek to leave a lasting impact on the world, long after they are gone. These individuals possess a unique ability to create meaningful and enduring legacies. Their hidden lives are characterized by a deep commitment to making a difference and leaving a positive mark on the world. From philanthropists to cultural icons, these legacy makers shape the future with their lasting contributions. Their stories are a testament to the power of creating a legacy and the impact of leaving a positive mark on the world.

Legacy makers often focus on initiatives that have a long-term impact, such as education, healthcare, and social justice. They understand that creating a legacy takes time and effort, and they are willing to invest in causes that will benefit future generations. Their stories highlight the importance of thinking beyond the present and the value of making a lasting contribution. Through their efforts, they create legacies that inspire and uplift others. Their hidden lives reveal a deep-seated passion for making a difference and a commitment to creating a better future.

As we explore the lives of these legacy makers, we gain insights into the qualities that set them apart. Their ability to envision a better future, their dedication to making a lasting impact, and their commitment to creating meaningful legacies are qualities that we can all aspire to. Their stories remind us that we all have the potential to leave a positive mark on the world. By looking beyond the balance sheet, we can uncover the hidden lives of those who shape the world through their lasting contributions.

In this chapter, we celebrate the legacy makers who create meaningful and enduring legacies. Their stories offer a glimpse into the hidden lives of those who dedicate themselves to making a lasting impact on the world. Through their efforts, they make a significant impact on the world. By recognizing and appreciating their contributions, we can foster a culture of legacy-building and long-term thinking that benefits everyone.

Beyond the Balance Sheet: The Hidden Lives of Those Who Shape the World

In a world often dominated by financial figures and balance sheets, there's a hidden narrative waiting to be discovered. "Beyond the Balance Sheet" unravels the untold stories of remarkable individuals who shape our world not through numbers, but through passion, perseverance, and an unyielding drive to make a difference.

This book takes readers on an inspiring journey through the lives of visionary dreamers, unsung heroes, ethical innovators, relentless problem-solvers, and fearless risk-takers. It celebrates the quiet strategists, resilient survivors, inspirational leaders, and creative pioneers who push the boundaries of what is possible. With each chapter, you'll dive deep into the world of humble innovators, persistent advocates, respected mentors, and community builders who connect and uplift others.

As you explore the lives of these extraordinary individuals, you'll gain insights into the qualities that set them apart and learn valuable lessons about resilience, collaboration, creativity, and legacy-building. "Beyond the Balance Sheet" reveals the profound impact that these hidden lives have on our society and inspires readers to look beyond the surface to find the true value in themselves and those around them.

Join us on this captivating exploration of the human spirit, and discover the hidden lives of those who shape the world in ways that numbers alone can never capture. This book is a celebration of the power of dreams, the strength of character, and the enduring legacy of those who dare to make a difference.

www.ingramcontent.com/pod-product-compliance
Lightning Source LLC
LaVergne TN
LVHW020457080526
838202LV00057B/6008